THE ELEPHANT SEAL

BY
WILLIAM R. SANFORD
CARL R. GREEN

EDITED BY
DR. HOWARD SCHROEDER, Ph.D.
Professor in Reading and Language Arts
Dept. of Curriculum and Instruction
Mankato State University

CRESTWOOD HOUSE
Mankato, Minnesota

LIBRARY OF CONGRESS CATALOGING IN PUBLICATION DATA

Sanford, William R. (William Reynolds).
The elephant seal.

(Wildlife, habits & habitat)
Includes index.
SUMMARY: Describes the physical characteristics, habits, and natural environment of the elephant seal.
1. Elephant seals--Juvenile literature. [1. Elephant seals. 2. Seals (Animals)] I. Green, Carl R. II. Schroeder, Howard. III. Title. IV. Series.
QL737.P64S35   1987   599.74'8   87-22349
ISBN 0-89686-330-1

International Standard Book Number:	Library of Congress Catalog Card Number:
Library Binding 0-89686-330-1	87-22349

CREDITS

Illustrations:
Cover Photo: Animals Animals © Joe and Carol McDonald
Animals Animals © Bradley Smith: 4
N. H. Cheatham/DRK Photo: 7
Erwin and Peggy Bauer: 8, 19, 23, 28, 40, 43
Brad Smith/Hillstrom Stock Photo: 11
M. P. Kahl/DRK Photo: 12
Gary R. Zahm/DRK Photo: 15
Anthony Mercieca/Hillstrom Stock Photo: 16, 39
Animals Animals © E. R. Degginger: 20
Animals Animals © Doug Allan: 24-25
Jeff Foott/DRK Photo: 26, 36, 44
Lynn Rogers: 33
Andy Schlabach: 45
Graphic Design & Production:
Baker Street Productions, Ltd.

CRESTWOOD HOUSE
Hwy. 66 South, Box 3427
Mankato, MN 56002-3427

TABLE OF CONTENTS

Anne studied the tiny offshore island through field glasses. As she watched, a huge sea creature hauled itself out of the water. It moved up the rocky beach like a clumsy caterpillar. "Maybe it's a walrus," she told herself. Then she saw the trunk-like nose. "That's an elephant seal!" she said.

Elephant seals are large and clumsy.

An Año Nuevo State Reserve ranger was standing close by. "Yes, the big bulls are coming ashore for the breeding season," the ranger said. "That looks like Abe, but I can't be sure. When I go over there tomorrow I'll check the tag on his hind flipper."

"Let me take a look," Anne's brother begged, tugging at the field glasses. After focusing them, Alex exclaimed, "Wow! I didn't know seals grew that big. How much does Abe weigh?"

The California ranger's name was Donna. "Abe is about as big as these northern elephant seals get," she said. "I'd guess his weight at four thousand pounds (1,814 kg) and his length at sixteen feet (4.9 m). He's come in early to stake his claim to that stretch of beach."

Anne was thinking that Abe weighed more than her entire class back at school. Then she had another thought. "How can you tell one elephant seal from another?" she asked. "It must be like trying to tell one overstuffed sausage from another."

Donna chuckled. "Two marine biologists worked with us on that problem. Elephant seals aren't vicious, but the bulls will attack if they think you're a threat to their cows. You have to mark them so that each bull can be identified from a distance."

"I'd throw balloons filled with paint at them," Alex said.

"That was the second idea the biologists tried," Donna told him. "Their first idea was to fill a fire extinguisher with black dye. That was a good plan — until the spray hit the first bull. He woke up and charged us. You don't know how fast you can run until you've been chased by two tons of angry elephant seal!"

"What did you try next?" Alex wondered.

"We filled plastic bags with waterproof paint," Donna went on. "Then we bombed each seal with a different color. After that, we called them by initials such as YLN or RRS. YLN stands for 'Yellow on Left side of Neck'. Can you guess what RRS means?"

"That must be 'Red on Right Side'," Anne said quickly.

"Right you are," Donna said with a smile. "The paint bombs worked, but they were pretty messy. Later on, we found a way to mark the bulls with a bleach made from hydrogen peroxide. The scientists painted foot-high letters on the bulls' backs while they were sleeping. The letters bleached the seals' hair quite nicely. After we finished, I could read Abe's name from more than a hundred feet (30 m) away."

Alex looked puzzled. "I can't see any letters on Abe's back," he said.

"Elephant seals grow new coats each spring," Donna explained. "That's why we also put a plastic tag on Abe's rear flipper. In a few days, we'll go out to the island to bleach him again."

6

Anne heard her father calling. She turned to the ranger. "Thanks for telling us about Abe," she said. "Elephant seals may not be pretty, but they sure are interesting!"

Elephant seals won't win any beauty contests, but they're always fun to watch!

CHAPTER ONE:

Thousands of years ago, a land carnivore began spending more and more time in the sea. Scientists believe the animal was related to the ancestors of today's dogs and bears. Over the centuries, this animal developed into a superb swimmer and diver. Its body adapted to a new life in the water.

Even though these animals returned to the ocean, they were still mammals. They were warm-blooded and they gave birth to live young. Unlike the whales

The "fin-footed" elephant seal has adapted to life on land as well as in the water.

8

and dolphins, however, they returned to the land to give birth. Today, their descendants are called the *Pinnipedia,* the "fin-footed ones." People know them better as seals, sea lions, and walruses.

Seals and sea lions differ in several ways. A true seal's hind flippers can't turn forward, so it "walks" by hitching itself along with its body and its front flippers. A sea lion can walk — and even do an awkward gallop — on four flippers. You can also tell true seals from sea lions by looking at the animal's ears. Seals don't have external ears; sea lions do.

Two species of elephant seals

The elephant seal is a true seal, a member of the family *Phocoidea.* Other members of this family include the harp seal, the harbor seal, and the leopard seal. The elephant seal's family is made up of just two species, the northern and southern elephant seal. These two seals have slightly different teeth, skulls, and growth patterns. They behave in similar ways, however. The northern elephant seal *(Mirounga angustirostris)* is smaller, but it has a longer trunk. It breeds along the western coast of California and Mexico. The southern elephant seal *(Mirounga leo-*

nina) can be found on islands that lie in a great circle around Antarctica.

In both species, the males (known as bulls) grow much larger than the females (called cows). Southern bulls are the largest of the pinnipeds. These massive seals sometimes reach twenty-two feet (6.7 m) in length and six tons (5,443 kg) in weight. A weight of four tons (3,630 kg) is about average. Northern bulls seldom grow longer than sixteen feet (4.9 m). They weigh in at three to four thousand pounds (1,361-1,814 kg). The cows of both species are similar in size. A typical cow is eight feet (2.4 m) long and weighs two thousand pounds (907 kg).

Scarred skin and thick blubber

Northern elephant bulls all have a basic coat of grey-brown. This turns to a warmer yellow-brown before the yearly molt, when the seals grow a new coat. The older bulls often carry heavy scars on their chests and necks from fighting. This makes their wrinkled skin look even more cracked and tough than it really is. The cows tend to be a lighter grey-brown in tone, while elephant seal pups are born with a black, wooly coat. Adults have a coat of short, stiff hair. They lack the rich undercoat of the fur seal.

Seal hunters killed elephant seals for their fat, not their fur. The seal needs this layer of fat (called blubber) to protect it from the cold. Blubber also helps streamline the animal for faster movement in the water. Elephant seals build up an average of three inches (7.6 cm) of blubber on their bodies. Only the flippers lack this insulation. Pups are born without a thick layer of blubber. But they build up this layer of fat quickly because the cows produce milk with a high fat content.

A three-inch (7.6 cm) layer of blubber protects the elephant seal from the cold and helps it swim faster.

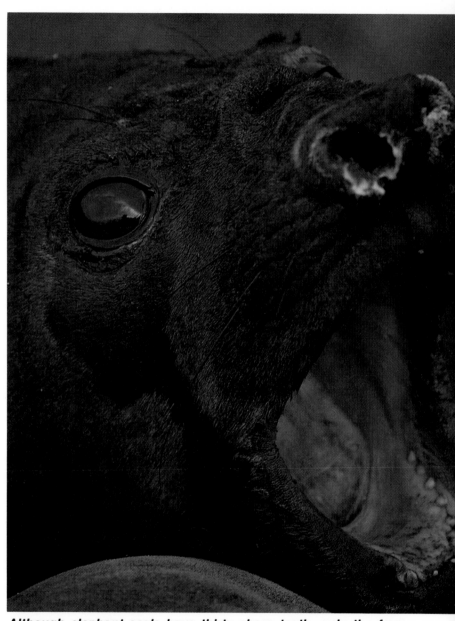

Although elephant seals have thirty sharp teeth, only the four canines are of much use.

12

Teeth for biting and a trunk for roaring

Elephant seals have thirty sharp, widely spaced teeth. Except for the four canines (ripping teeth), their teeth are of little value. The long, sharp canines are the bull's chief weapon in his battles with other bulls. The other teeth are good for catching prey, but not for chewing. Since it swallows its food whole, the seal probably hasn't developed a strong sense of taste.

The elephant seal's trunk is its most notable feature. Only the bulls grow this weird-looking nose. When he's excited, a bull inflates his trunk by tightening muscles and sending blood to the tissues. A northern bull's twelve-inch (30 cm) trunk hangs down over his mouth when it's relaxed. When he puffs it up, the trunk swells to twice its usual size.

The elephant seal's trunk isn't at all like an elephant's trunk. Naturalists believe its main purpose is to magnify the bull's roar. When a northern bull roars, he places the trunk inside his mouth. Then he gives a mighty series of snorts, with the mouth serving as an echo chamber. Southern bulls use their smaller trunks to deepen and magnify roars that start in their throats. The roar warns other bulls to stay away from the dominant bull's females.

The elephant seal's harsh, rhythmic roar is unique in the animal kingdom. The powerful sound carries for a mile (1.6 km) or more. People have a hard time describing it. Some have compared it to a backfiring car, others to cannonballs smashing a wooden fence. Naturalists can pick out a bull's breeding grounds by its roar. The bulls of San Nicolas Island, for example, sound off at twice the rate of Año Nuevo bulls.

All-purpose flippers

The elephant seal's flippers are highly modified legs and paws. The bones of all four legs are inside the seal's body. In the water, the powerful rear flippers propel the seal at speeds up to twelve miles (20 km) per hour. The front flippers are used as rudders for changing direction. On land, the elephant seal is as clumsy as it is agile in the water. The rear flippers are useless for walking. To move, the seal rocks backward and then lunges forward like a huge caterpillar. It extends its front flippers to help with balance.

The elephant seal's flippers have five digit bones, similar to those in your own hands. A flexible webbing connects the digits, and each digit has a sharp

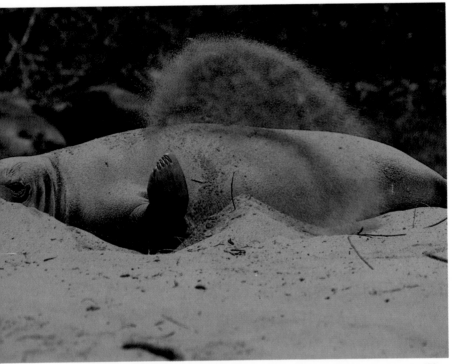

An elephant seal uses its flippers to throw sand over its back. The sand keeps the animal cool and protects it from insects.

flipper claw. The first and fifth digits are longer than the others. As with all true seals, the elephant seal's flippers have hair on both sides. The flippers look stiff, but a seal can twist its front flippers around to scratch the top of its head. The flippers are also good for throwing sand onto the seal's back. A layer of sand keeps away insects and guards against sunburn.

On land, an elephant seal sees only upright, moving objects.
Underwater, however, it sees very well.

Senses that work better underwater

Elephant seals have well-developed senses that work better in water than on land. Their large, round eyes see well in the dim light of the undersea world. On land, their eyes provide sharp images only in bright light. In dim light, they see objects as blurs. In addition, they tend to see only upright, moving objects. Thus, naturalists get close to elephant seals by slowly crawling toward them on their stomachs.

Although they don't have external ears, elephant seals hear well. Sounds carry better in water than in air, and the seals pick up the quietest of sounds. In addition, each elephant seal has long whiskers next to its mouth. Naturalists believe that the seal uses both its ears and whiskers to find food when it's diving in deep, murky water. The seal "reads" the vibrations it picks up as the size and location of its prey.

The elephant seal also has a keen sense of smell and touch. For example, a cow can tell her own pup from among a hundred others by its scent. As for touch, elephant seals crowd together even when there's plenty of room on the beach. Perhaps that's because they live solitary lives when they're in the sea. When they reach their beach habitats, they seem to want the feeling of being close to each other.

CHAPTER TWO:

For many months of the year, the elephant seal's favorite beaches lie deserted. The seals feed many miles offshore. Then instinct sends the seals back to the beaches where they were born. Both northern and southern elephant seals follow a calendar that brings them to shore twice a year.

Two widely separated ranges

The two species occupy habitats on opposite sides of the equator. The southern elephant seal lives in the cold waters around Antarctica. Some of the largest colonies can be found on the islands of Southern Georgia, the Falklands, Punta Norte, Prince Edward, and Macquarie. Almost half of them breed on South Georgia, which is east of Argentina. Another huge colony breeds on remote Macquarie. This island lies southeast of Australia on the edge of the Antarctic pack ice.

In 1907, the northern elephant seal was almost extinct. A colony of fewer than one hundred seals held on at Guadalupe Island off the coast of Baja California. However, the northern elephant seal has slowly recovered. Today, its breeding range reaches as far north as the Farallon Islands near San Francisco. The southern limit is Natividad Island, halfway down the Baja California peninsula. Single seals have been seen far north and south of these limits.

A diet of fish and squid

Elephant seals are carnivores that live on slow-swimming fish, squid, and small shellfish. Southern seals favor squid, while northern seals feast on small sharks, skates, and ratfish. Because they swallow

An elephant seal's long whiskers help it find food in deep water.

their prey whole, the seals need extra-long intestines to digest it. One elephant seal's intestine was measured at 662 feet (202 m).

Naturalists guess that the seals eat large amounts of food during the months they're at sea. They must build up good reserves of fat because they don't eat while they're on land. The diet of captive elephant seals gives a measure of their appetite. At a marine park in France, a one-ton (907 kg) bull named Henri eats seventy pounds (32 kg) of fish a day!

When an elephant seal dives, it closes its nostrils to prevent water from entering its lungs.

Deep-diving mammals

Finding ratfish in the elephant seal's diet surprised the naturalists. A seal must dive below three hundred feet (91 m) to catch this species. Actually, elephant seals can dive much deeper than that. The deepest dive of an elephant seal ever recorded is a thousand feet (305 m). At that depth, the water is dark and cold. The seal's sensitive eyes and ears help it find its prey. A thick layer of blubber keeps out the cold.

On these deep dives, the elephant seal's body easily handles pressures that human divers could not endure. As it dives, the seal empties its lungs of air. This keeps nitrogen bubbles from forming in the blood when it returns to the surface. Water can't enter its lungs because it closes its nostrils. If the seal opens its mouth to grab a fish, strong muscles seal off the opening to the lungs.

The elephant seal's heartbeat slows down during the dive. Less oxygen is sent to outlying parts of the body, although the blood itself does carry extra oxygen. Twelve percent of a seal's body weight is blood, compared to seven percent in a human body. This system allows the elephant seal to stay underwater for fifteen minutes or longer. When it surfaces, a few quick breaths replace the used-up oxygen and the seal is ready to dive again.

Two yearly visits to the land

Elephant seals visit the land twice each year. The first trip is for breeding purposes. The second trip is for molting. Northern elephant seals give birth to their young in December and January. After the pups are weaned in March and April, mating begins. The colony returns in May to begin the yearly molt. Southern elephant seals reverse the seasons. They breed from August to October, and molt in December.

At the start of the breeding season, the bulls take up their positions on the beaches. Here they fight to hold on to their territory and the females that gather there. The bull that wins the battles becomes the beachmaster. His group of females is called a harem. Each beachmaster mates with as many cows as he can control. An average harem contains ten to fifteen cows, but a few beachmasters guard even larger harems. The younger bulls hang out on the edges of the harem. If a young cow strays away, they try to mate with her in the water.

Molting and sleeping

Life in the colony is different during the molting season. The seals crawl up on the beach and lie

Two bulls fight for the position of "beachmaster."

together in great smelly piles. They snort, yawn, grunt, and cough. Fighting is rare during this period. The seals prefer muddy wallows that seem to soothe their itchy skin. As they molt, the skin and hair drop off in large patches. As with the breeding season, the seals go without food during these forty days. Naturalists who visit a molting colony report that the smell is almost unbearable.

The seals lie in great smelly heaps as they go through the forty-day molting season.

While they're molting, elephant seals do a lot of heavy sleeping. Scientists can measure a sleeping seal's temperature, heart rate, and breathing without waking it up. When they first did this, they were surprised to find that the seals sometimes forget to breathe. They breathe normally for five minutes, and then they don't breathe for another five minutes. Seals have also been seen sleeping in the water. By controlling their buoyancy (the tendency to float), they can sleep anywhere between the surface and the bottom of a shallow bay.

The elephant seal can sleep just about anywhere.

Too big for most predators

Elephant seals are too big for most predators to tackle. On land, they breed on island beaches where large carnivores are unknown. In the sea, killer whales and leopard seals do kill a few pups. Sharks don't seem to be a big problem, but seals have been found with scars left by shark bites on their hides. The big bulls fight for mates, but seldom kill each other.

The first few months of life are the most dangerous. The biggest danger to the pups comes from the huge bulls. When a bull charges an intruder, he crushes any pup that doesn't move out of his way. Females will also bite a pup that annoys them. An unusual accident happens to southern pups who lie out on a snowy beach. If the weather turns warm, their body heat may be great enough to melt the snow under them. Trapped in a pit, they may starve before they can escape.

As with other wild animals, elephant seals suffer from a variety of accidents and parasites. If a seal swallows a jagged piece of rock, it may block the stomach and kill the animal. Most seals also carry tapeworms, roundworms, and thorny-headed worms that cause tumors. Ticks and lice infest the skin, especially when the elephant seals are out of the water.

Naturalists can tell a seal's age from the rings of dentine and cement in its teeth. By this measure, the oldest bull on record lived only twenty years. The cows live only ten or twelve years. That's not many yearly cycles of feeding, breeding, and molting for such a large animal.

It would take a very brave predator to attack this elephant seal bull!

CHAPTER THREE:

December and January are busy months on California's Channel Islands. The northern elephant seals are arriving to begin their breeding season. Several naturalists are already living in a tent on San Nicolas Island. They're armed with cameras, tape recorders, and a supply of bleach.

Dawn and Chris Hope are a husband-and-wife team. They paint a three-letter name on the back of each seal in one colony. As each bull arrives, he gets a name. The painting goes smoothly until Dawn backs away from one bull and steps on another's flipper. The second bull rears up above her, mouth open and canines flashing. His deep, pulsing roar drowns out the sound of the surf. Dawn spins around and hurries to safety. Satisfied, the bull lies down for another nap.

Mac defends his title

The fights for dominance begin as soon as the bulls drag themselves up on shore. In this colony, Mac has won the role of beachmaster. But each bull that arrives is a new test of his status. Mac's long and bloody fight with Bum is typical.

Mac greets Bum's challenge with an ear-splitting series of roars. Bum responds with his own loud roar. The two great bulls meet chest-to-chest. Rearing up almost eight feet (2.4 m), they rock back and forth. Each tries to bite the other's neck while also protecting his delicate trunk. Suddenly, Mac slashes downward and bites into Bum's neck. Blood spurts as the younger bull pulls back. Still, Bum won't give up. He charges back and gets in several rips of his own.

The fight ends in a strange way. As he swings his head to land a blow, Bum's trunk flops downward. Before he can stop himself, he's bitten his own nose! This is too much. Bloody and defeated, Bum turns to leave. Mac is equally bloody, but he seals his victory by biting Bum's rear flipper.

The cows give birth

The cows come ashore in late December and early January. Kae and twenty other cows join Mac's harem, but they refuse to have anything to do with him. Their attention is turned to the coming birth of their pups.

Kae's male pup is born a week later. Fuz is four feet (1.2 m) long and weighs ninety pounds (41 kg). He finds her teats and begins nursing within a few hours of his birth. Kae's rich milk is fifty-five percent butterfat. Fuz will gain almost eight pounds (3.6 kg) a day! In a week he'll double his birth weight, and he'll double it again before he's weaned.

Harem life is hard for the black, wooly pups. Today, Mac suddenly roars and moves out to repel a younger bull. Fuz barely escapes his blind, steamroller charge. Next to him, a cow rolls over and pins a squealing pup beneath her crushing weight. Pups that lose their mothers are in danger, too. Starving for milk, they turn into milk thieves. If a cow discovers that she's nursing a strange pup, she gives it a painful bite. The orphans die unless they find a foster mother who has lost her own pup.

Harem life is hectic

Kae nurses Fuz for only twenty-seven days. After that, she refuses to let the pup take her teat. The cow's instincts are telling her it's time to mate. Mac has been waiting for this day. He mates with Kae several times a day during the next week. Soon, only a month after she gave birth, Kae is pregnant again. The egg she carries in her body doesn't start growing until two months have passed. In that way, Kae's pregnancy will end on schedule a year from now.

Mac is fourteen years old and a beachmaster for the first time. He'll try to hold his position next year, but another bull may beat him out. Even now, he's weary from the task of fighting and mating. Every time Mac turns around, a young bull is sneaking in to try to mate with one of his cows. With an angry roar, Mac races to defend his rights.

None of the adult seals have eaten since they reached the beach. They've been living on the fat they stored up in the months at sea. As the pups are weaned, the cows go back to the water to feed. The pups cannot join them until they finish molting. Living on stored-up fat, Fuz and the others wallow in the mud to ease their itching skin. Dawn and Chris spend some time with the playful pups. Fuz likes to be rolled over and over, like a roly-poly doll.

Because they've stopped nursing, the pups are known as weaners. They finish their molt in the middle of March. Fuz now wears the shiny, silvery grey-brown coat of the adult elephant seal. Each day the weaners make trips into the water to catch small crabs and other easy prey. No one teaches them how to swim. The waves wash up the bodies of weaners who drown trying to learn.

Fuz is one of the lucky ones. When he leaves the island in May, he's a skillful diver and swimmer. In the water he discovers the joy of being nearly weight-

Without anyone to teach them, these young weaners learn how to swim and catch fish.

less. With only instinct to guide him, he swims northward along the coast. For the next seven months, he divides his time between deep water and an island off northern California. The fishing is good and Fuz catches his fill of fish and squid.

The colony returns to molt and to breed

In May the colony returns to San Nicolas. This time Dawn and Chris must endure the odor created by molting elephant seals. The seals gather together in great piles. Crowding in close to each other helps them stay warm.

Mac flops into the middle of a mud wallow. His skin and hair flake off in large patches. As each seal completes its molt, it slips back into the water. Mac is among the last to leave. The biggest bulls take the longest to finish their molt. Finally, the beach is empty again.

The calendar turns to December. Like clockwork, the big bulls crawl up on the beach once again. Mac comes back to fight for his harem, but his luck has run out. This year, Bum takes away his status as beachmaster. This is Mac's last chance. In human terms, he's "over the hill" at fifteen.

Fuz comes back, too. He won't be old enough to mate until he's four. But four-year-olds don't have much chance against mature bulls like Mac and Bum. These young bulls wait offshore, hoping to mate with a young cow before she reaches the beach. Fuz joins the playful one-year-olds in a separate colony. Their favorite game is surfing the waves that break on the beach.

Each year, Fuz and the other young bulls will return to this beach. When they're old enough, they'll join the endless battle for mates. Some will never win a harem, but Fuz will go on to father dozens of new pups. That's the way of life for this largest of all pinnipeds.

CHAPTER FOUR:

How could anyone kill an elephant seal? The huge creatures aren't pretty, but they have a charm all their own. Their soft brown eyes seem to say, "Please leave us alone." In the 1800's, no one listened to their plea. People needed oil, and the elephant seal's blubber was a good source.

The hunting begins

In 1775, the famous Captain Cook discovered the remote South Atlantic island of South Georgia. The island was a favorite breeding ground for pinnipeds. Along with fur seals and sea lions, Cook found large colonies of southern elephant seals.

The first seal hunters who followed Captain Cook didn't bother the elephant seals. They were most interested in the fur seals. Over the next forty-five years, ships made yearly trips to South Georgia and other islands to hunt fur seals. The killing was beyond imagination. In seven years, the seal hunters took three million skins on the island of Masafuera.

As fur seals grew scarce, the hunters began to kill the elephant seals. The skins were useless, but each

Until the late 1800's, elephant seals were killed for the high-quality oil in their blubber.

giant seal was a walking oil drum. The blubber from a large southern bull provided as much as two hundred gallons (757 liters) of high-quality oil. The smaller females yielded about eighty gallons (303 liters).

Better yet, the hunters learned, the seals were easy game. The men began a hunt by lining up on the beach where they could cut off any escape into the sea. Then they drove the seals inland, where they killed them with clubs, lances, and guns. If the bulls panicked, so much the better. In the crush that followed, the huge males helped the hunters by killing their own cows and pups.

The same careless greed led whaling crews to the breeding grounds of the northern elephant seals. Entire colonies were wiped out along the Pacific coast. The mass killing pushed both species of elephant seals close to extinction. With the seals almost gone, hunting stopped in the late 1800's. Naturalists feared that the northern elephant seal was lost forever.

The southern elephant seals recovered after the hunting stopped. By 1910, the colonies had grown large enough to make hunting profitable again. This time, Great Britain limited the number of kills on South Georgia. Between 1910 and 1964, seal hunters were licensed to take only six thousand elephant seals a year. As time went on, it became clear that the world didn't really need seal oil. Finally, in 1964, the British government put a stop to all hunting.

The elephant seal in captivity

While seal hunters went about their bloody business, the elephant seal became a popular zoo animal. The Hamburg Zoo in Germany put a southern elephant seal on display in 1910. This same zoo later amazed visitors with a bull named Goliath. The name was well chosen, for Goliath weighed almost five thousand pounds (2,268 kg). Feeding him took a hundred pounds (45 kg) of fish a day. On one day, the big bull gulped down 385 pounds (175 kg) of fish. The popular Goliath came to a sad and painful end. He died after swallowing a broken bottle that someone threw into the seal's enclosure.

Zoos had trouble keeping their elephant seals alive. The Philadelphia Zoo put five pups on display in 1881, but all of them died. No one tried again until the New York Zoo showed another southern elephant seal in 1911. Slowly, the zookeepers learned to provide the proper living conditions. The San Diego Zoo has kept northern elephant seals since the 1920's. For many years, the zoo used a picture of an elephant seal on all of its advertising.

Breeding elephant seals in captivity was a tougher task. Most zoos can't afford to keep a large harem for their bulls. But the bulls become violent with only one or two females around. In 1965, a cow in the Stuttgart Zoo in Germany finally gave birth to a female pup named Isolde. The zookeepers raised Isolde themselves. The pup was doing well, but she died before her second birthday. An exam showed that Isolde had swallowed gravel that people threw into her enclosure.

If we're going to save our wildlife, we'll have to do better than we did for Isolde. The successful rescue of the northern elephant seal, however, shows us a happier picture. People and governments can create miracles when they work together.

CHAPTER FIVE:

In the early 1900's, naturalists said that the northern elephant seal was extinct. Year after year, none of the great pinnipeds showed up on their usual beaches.

The naturalists weren't far from wrong. Only one small colony survived. Fewer than a hundred elephant seals were still breeding on an island off the coast of Baja California. When scientists landed on Guadalupe Island in 1907, they stumbled on the remaining seals. The people in the expedition took pictures and shot several animals for display in museums.

Guadalupe Island is still "home" to many elephant seals.

The elephant seal refuses to give up

The odds were against them, but the seals didn't give up. Left alone on their remote island, the colony grew. By 1922, there were enough of them to attract seal hunters again. To prevent a new slaughter, the Mexican government passed a law that protected the elephant seal. Soldiers were kept on Guadalupe to prevent poaching. It was a lonely job for the soldiers, but they kept the illegal seal hunters away.

Today, the colony at Año Nuevo produces as many as 1,400 pups each year.

40

Within ten years, small colonies appeared off the California coast. The United States joined Mexico in banning all hunting of the endangered species. Before long, breeding colonies were seen on the Channel Islands of San Miguel, San Nicolas, and Santa Barbara. Despite this movement, nine out of ten elephant seals still breed on Baja California's Guadalupe and San Benito islands.

The population spreads to Año Nuevo

In 1955, elephant seals landed on the island of Año Nuevo for the first time in a century. This eight-acre (3.2 hectare) island lies only a few hundred yards off the northern California coast. In 1957, the state of California set aside the island and a thousand acres (400 hectares) of the mainland shore as an elephant-seal preserve. Strong tides and dangerous currents keep casual visitors from disturbing the seals.

The elephant seals share Año Nuevo with harbor seals and sea lions. As with other populations, the biggest bulls have the biggest harems. Over eighty percent of the cows mate with only four percent of the bulls. The colony produces about 1,400 pups each year. Rangers estimate that five out of six pups survive to become weaners.

Thanks to this type of conservation, the northern elephant seal is no longer endangered. The population has grown from fewer than a hundred to more than one hundred thousand. Better yet, their number is doubling every five years. However, naturalists fear that other dangers lie in wait for the elephant seal.

Good news and bad news

The good news for the northern elephant seal is that the population has recovered. Laws that protect the elephant seal and other pinnipeds are being enforced. The public seems to care about these animals. Taxpayers are willing to support wildlife preserves such as Año Nuevo.

The bad news is still waiting to happen. One threat comes from the federal government. The Department of the Interior wants to let oil companies drill for oil off the California coast. No one knows what a major oil spill might do to the Channel Islands and their wildlife. In addition, oil exploration would bring ocean traffic and drilling rigs to the channel.

Naturalists think the noise and confusion might upset the breeding cycle of the elephant seal.

Another danger comes from commercial fishers. As the seal population grows, the seals eat more fish and squid. Most of the species they eat aren't caught as food fish. Even so, the fishers complain that seals rob them of their profits. This fight hasn't become serious yet. But history shows that animals seldom win in a battle over a limited resource.

Finally, elephant seals face a problem naturalists call the "genetic bottleneck". Northern elephant

The elephant seal still faces many dangers, including oil spills, commercial fishers, and epidemic diseases.

seals, they remind us, are all descended from the bulls of Guadalupe Island. In addition, a small number of bulls father most of the pups each year. Thus, most northern elephant seals carry the same genes. What affects one elephant seal will likely affect them all. If the climate changes, or if a new disease should strike, the entire population might be wiped out in a short time.

The northern elephant seal disappeared from the California waters once before. No one wants to see that happen again.

The beaches of California and Mexico would seem very empty without these huge, fascinating creatures.

MAP:

The shaded area shows the habitat of the northern elephant seal.

INDEX/GLOSSARY:

INDEX/GLOSSARY:

If you would like to know more about all kinds of wildlife, you should take a look at the other books in this series.

You'll find books on bald eagles and other birds. Books on alligators and other reptiles. There are books about deer and other big-game animals. And there are books about sharks and other creatures that live in the ocean.

In all of the books you will learn that life in the wild is not easy. But you will also learn what people can do to help wildlife survive. So read on!